START-UP▲
BLUES GUITAR
It's never been easier to start playing blues guitar!

Published by
Wise Publications
14-15 Berners Street, London W1T 3LJ, UK.

Exclusive Distributors:
Music Sales Limited
Distribution Centre, Newmarket Road, Bury St Edmunds, Suffolk IP33 3YB, UK.
Music Sales Pty Limited
20 Resolution Drive, Caringbah, NSW 2229, Australia.

Order No. AM1002936
ISBN: 978-1-84938-984-6
This book © Copyright 2011 Wise Publications, a division of Music Sales Limited.

Adapted by David Harrison from an original book by Darryl Winston.
Produced by Shedwork.com
Design by Fresh Lemon.
Photography by Matthew Ward.
Models: Sagat Guirey and David Weston.
Edited by Tom Farncombe.
Printed in the EU.

With thanks to the City Lit, London.

www.musicsales.com

WISE PUBLICATIONS
part of The Music Sales Group
London / New York / Paris / Sydney / Copenhagen / Berlin / Madrid / Hong Kong / Tokyo

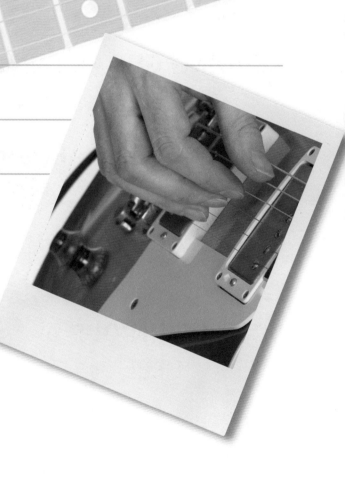

The guitar is the single most important instrument in the history of the blues—and it continues to define the sound of blues and rock today.

The instrument's versatility and expressive power make it a natural choice for blues improvisation—and a superb complement to the human voice.

In fact, the blues began as a vocal form, which grew out of the work songs and spirituals sung by African-American slaves.

Early blues guitarists discovered how to use techniques such as slides, bends and vibrato to imitate blues singers. With this exciting new vocabulary, together with a strong sense of personal style, they brought the instrument—and the blues itself—to new heights of expression.

Whether you are a beginning guitarist, or an experienced player, this easy instruction guide contains everything you need to know to master the basics of blues guitar.

You'll learn blues chords, progressions, and scales in every key—and explore classic blues fills, turnarounds, intros and endings.

You'll also get to create your own solos and riffs using important blues techniques, such as hammer-ons, pull-offs, slides and bends. Useful finger picking and strumming patterns are also provided, along with suggestions for developing your own blues accompaniments.

For easy reading, the examples and songs in this book are shown in both music notation and guitar tablature.

There are many different styles of blues, and you can play on any kind of guitar, whether electric or acoustic.

As you learn new blues patterns and techniques, you'll get to perform a variety of classic blues songs in different styles.

These songs are favourites of many great blues players, including Mississippi John Hurt, Blind Lemon Jefferson, Mance Lipscomb, Robert Johnson, Furry Lewis, Dave Van Ronk, Eric Clapton, Leadbelly and Woody Guthrie.

You will also find special sections on country, jazz and rock blues—and get a chance to explore some of the techniques used by the masters of these styles.

Once you are familiar with the basics of the blues, you will be able to play hundreds of new songs on your own. In fact, exploring new songs and techniques is the best way to develop your own personal playing style.

It also helps to listen to the work of the blues masters—and to create opportunities to practise and perform with other blues musicians.

BLUES CHORDS IN A

A basic blues requires only three chords—the I7, IV7 and V7 chords of a given major key.

These chords are built on the first, fourth, and fifth degrees of the major scale.

In a blues in the key of A major, the basic chords are A7, D7 and E7.

This is a favourite key of many blues guitarists because it is easy and natural-sounding.

The following chord diagrams show how these three chords are fingered on the guitar fretboard.

Guitarists will tell you that playing chords isn't difficult, it's *changing* between chords that can be tricky.

Moving from one shape to another needs special care and attention, so it's worth spending a moment looking at ways to make it easier.

Take a look at the three chord shapes on this page, and see if you can find any similarities between them. These similarities might not be obvious at first glance, but any common features that two chord shapes share can make it easier to move from one to the other.

For example, by comparing the A7 and D7 shapes, you can see that the notes on the second and fourth strings in the A7 shape are simply moved up to the first and third strings for the D7 shape.

In fact, you might like to play the A7 shape with the *second* finger on the fourth string to make that movement easier. Get the first finger ready to come down onto the 1st fret when you move over to D7.

As for E7, the first and second fingers are on the same frets as they are for D7. So, when you change from E7 to D7, keep these fingers over their respective frets as you move them over.

As you work through the book and expand your chord repertoire, you'll also see that certain chords tend to crop up with groups of other particular chords, so you'll begin to learn families of shapes.

This is especially true in the blues, where many, many songs just use the same three chords.

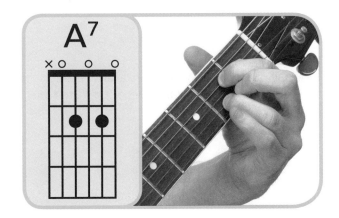

Practise playing these chords in this pattern, strumming each chord four times, as shown. Repeat this pattern several times, keeping a steady rhythm.

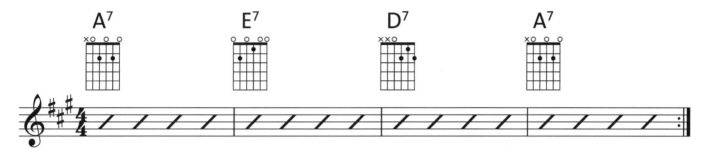

Strum once for each slash (/).

Once you can change from one chord to another smoothly and easily, try playing the 12-bar blues progression below.

This chord pattern is the basic form for thousands of standard blues songs.

Play this and get the sound of the chord changes in your head and you're well on the way to playing the blues!

Basic 12-Bar Blues Progression

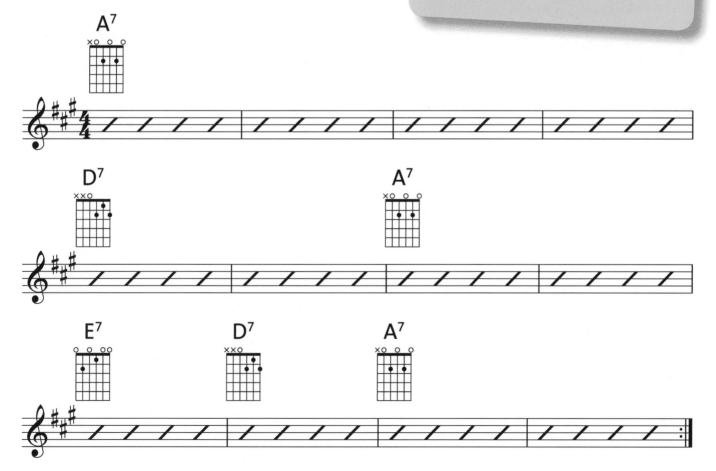

BLUES CHORDS IN E

In the key of E, the three basic blues chords are E7, A7 and B7, which are built on the first, fourth and fifth degrees of the E major scale. You are already familiar with the A7 and E7 chords. Play them again now along with the B7 chord.

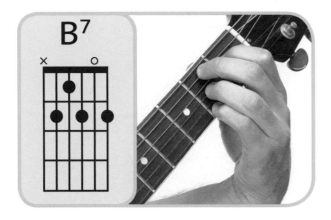

Practise playing these chords in this pattern, strumming each chord four times, as shown. Repeat this pattern several times in tempo.

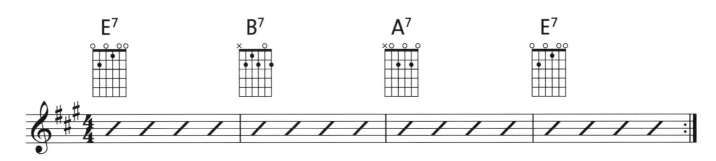

Once you can change from one chord to another smoothly and easily, try playing the 12-bar blues 'C.C. Rider' in the key of E (opposite).

This classic song was often performed by blues guitarists Mississippi John Hurt and Mance Lipscomb.

Also known as 'See See Rider', this traditional American blues became a chart hit for a wide range of blues, R&B and rock artists, including Ma Rainey (1925), Chuck Willis (1957), Lavern Baker (1963), and Eric Burdon & the Animals (1966).

C.C. Rider

E⁷

/ / / / / / / / / / / / / / /

C. C. Rid-er,   see what you have done.___   I said,

A⁷   E⁷

/ / / / / / / / / / / / / / /

C. C. Rid-er,   see what you have done.   Well, you

B⁷   A⁷   E⁷

/ / / / / / / / / / / / / / /

made me love you,   now your love is   gone.

2.
C.C. Rider, I need you by my side,
I said, C.C. Rider, I need you by my side.
You're the only one who keeps me satisfied.

3.
Goin' away, Rider, won't be back till fall,
Yes, I'm goin' away, Rider, won't be back till fall.
If I find some good love, won't be back at all.

STRUMMING CHORDS

Now that you've learned the blues chords in two important keys, get ready to play some different strumming patterns. Traditional blues guitarists use different finger style strums to add interest and movement to their playing. Until now, you have played four even strums per measure using down-strokes.

Try this on an A chord now.

You can make your accompaniment more interesting by adding up-strokes in between the four main down-strokes in each measure.

Whether you're using a pick, or playing finger-style, strum down and up on an A chord using this strumming pattern. The beat count below each stave will help you play the right rhythm pattern.

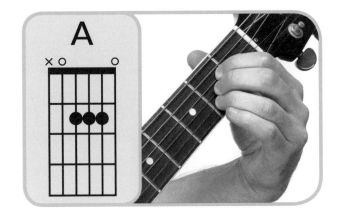

$\sqcap$ = *down-stroke*
$\lor$ = *up-stroke*

Here are three variations on this strum that you can use to add interest at different points in a blues song.

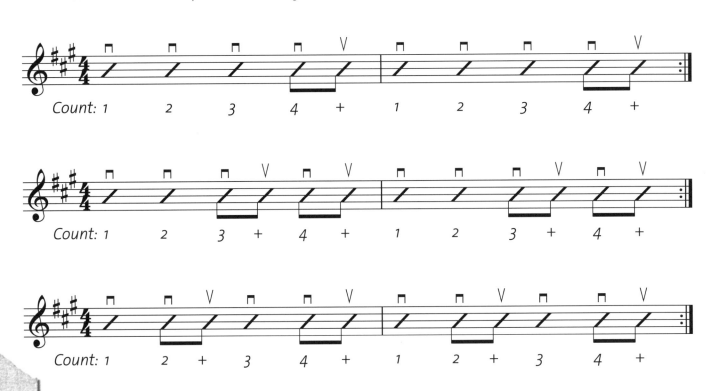

Now play 'Worried Man Blues' using the indicated strumming patterns. This old song is a particular favourite of bluegrass and country players—and features a 16-bar blues form (an extended version of the 12-bar blues).

Once you can play 'Worried Man Blues' smoothly as written, play the song a few more times and explore some strumming patterns of your own.

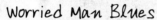

Worried Man Blues

It takes a wor-ried man to sing a wor-ried song, It

takes a wor-ried man to sing a wor-ried song, It

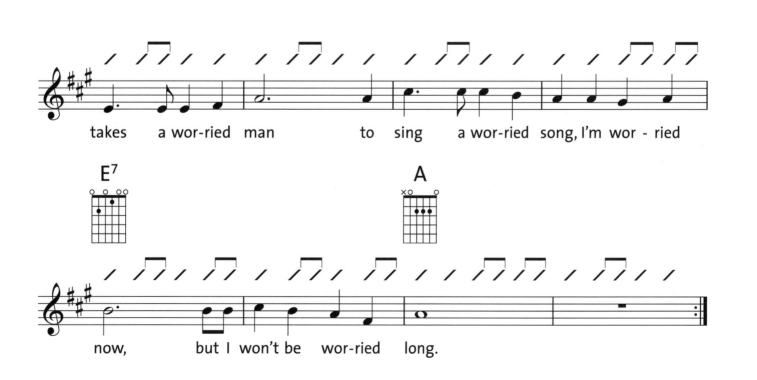

takes a wor-ried man to sing a wor-ried song, I'm wor-ried

now, but I won't be wor-ried long.

BASS-CHORD STRUMMING PATTERNS

Many blues guitarists use broken chords to add a hard-driving, rhythmic quality to their playing. The simplest broken-chord pattern is called the bass-chord strum. For this strum, play a single bass note on the first beat of each measure.

Then strum downwards on all the other strings three times in tempo. Try this pattern using the A7 and E7 chords shown.

Play the fifth string for the A7 chord bass note and the sixth string for the E7 chord bass note, as indicated. Repeat this pattern several times in tempo.

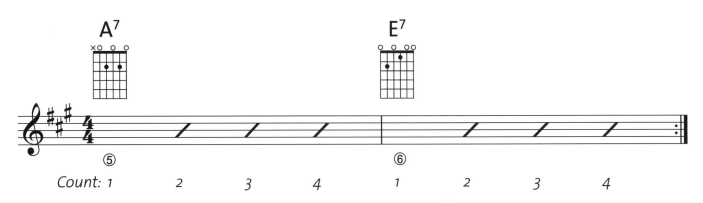

Now play 'Goin' Down That Road Feelin' Bad' using this pattern. This traditional blues song was made famous by Woody Guthrie—and is featured in the repertoire of many blues and country-blues musicians.

Like 'Worried Man Blues', this one has a 16-bar blues form. Feel free to sing the melody (or have a friend sing or play it) as you practise a steady bass-chord accompaniment.

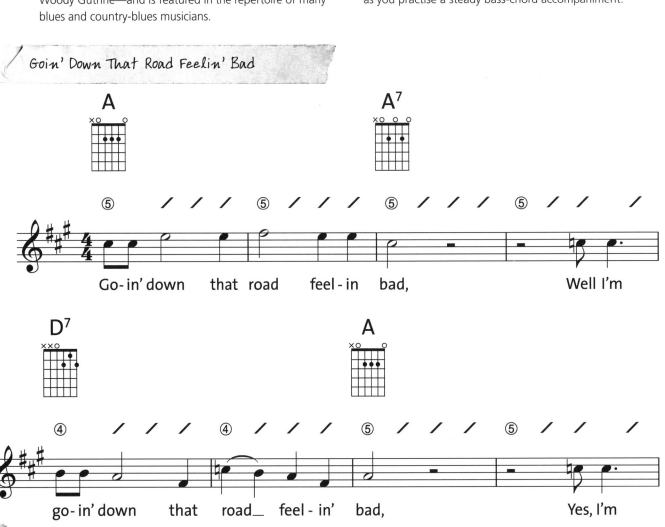

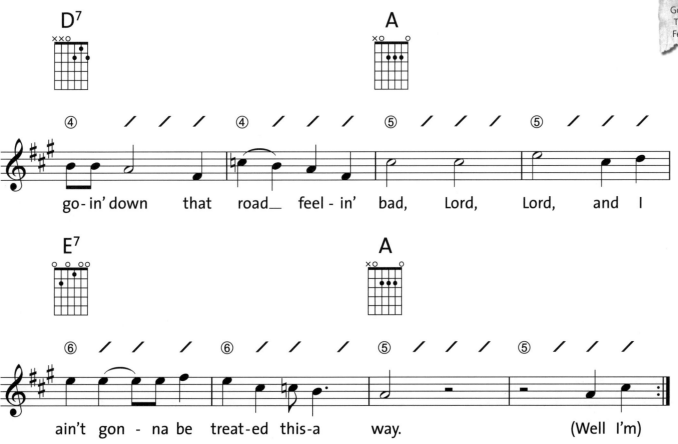

go-in' down   that   road__   feel - in'   bad,   Lord,   Lord,   and   I

ain't gon - na   be   treat-ed   this-a   way.   (Well I'm)

Once you can play 'Goin' Down That Road Feelin' Bad'
smoothly as written, play it through a few more times and
explore the following variations on the bass-chord strum.

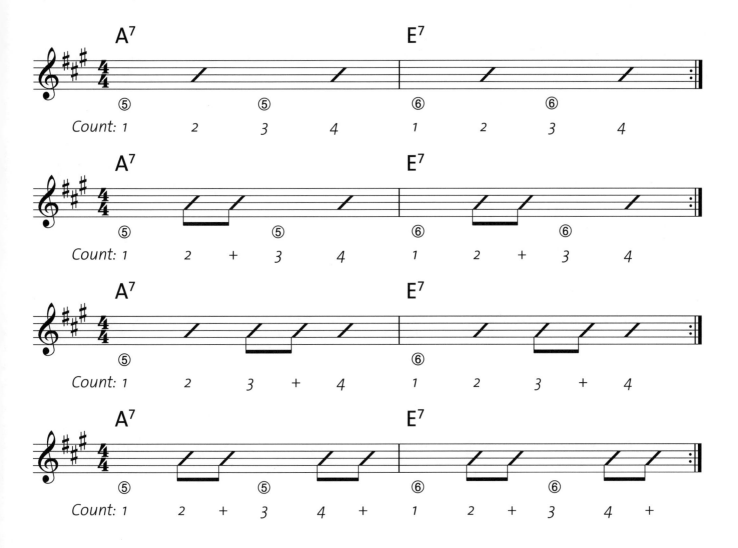

READING GUITAR TABLATURE

Tablature is a system of notation designed especially for guitarists. So that you can read the fills, turnarounds and solos that are covered later in this book, you'll need a basic grasp of how tablature (or tab) works.

The tablature staff is composed of six lines. Each line represents a string of the guitar, with the first string being the highest, and the sixth string, the lowest.

Look at the diagram below to see how the six strings are represented. As with standard notation, the lines are arranged in order of pitch, low to high.

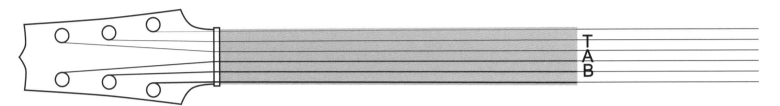

Fret numbers placed on the lines of guitar tablature tell you which fret to play on a given string (fret 1 is the fret nearest to the tuning pegs and 0 indicates an unfretted or open string).

When fingering numbers are included, they appear with the notes on the staff: 1 = index finger, 2 = middle, 3 = ring, and 4 = little.

The first position E minor pentatonic scale is shown below in music notation and guitar tablature. Play this descending scale several times in tempo.

Use your middle finger (2) for notes on the 2nd fret and your ring finger (3) for notes on the 3rd fret, as indicated. Play open strings where you see 0.

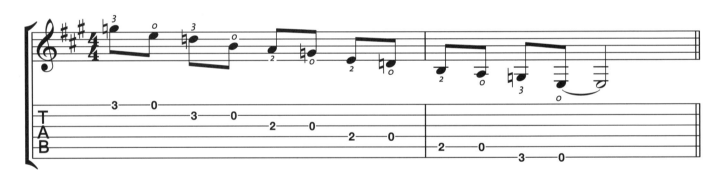

While guitar tablature shows you which frets and strings to play you must get the rhythm from the notes on the music staff.

Here are four standard note values and rests—and their relative duration in beats.

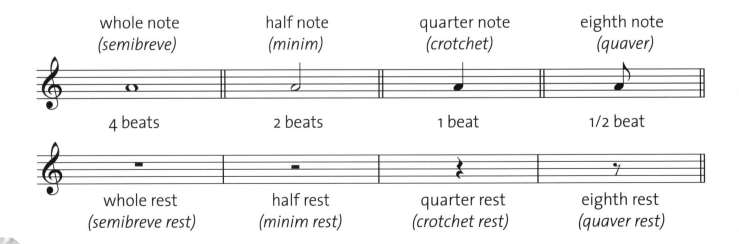

whole note *(semibreve)*	half note *(minim)*	quarter note *(crotchet)*	eighth note *(quaver)*
4 beats	2 beats	1 beat	1/2 beat
whole rest *(semibreve rest)*	half rest *(minim rest)*	quarter rest *(crotchet rest)*	eighth rest *(quaver rest)*

HAMMER-ONS, PULL-OFFS, SLIDES AND BENDS

Blues guitarists make great use of embellishments that come from deft left-hand finger movements. The four main techniques you'll need are listed here. You'll need to get these under your fingers to articulate blues guitar lines properly.

Hammer-on

A slur connecting two ascending notes indicates a hammer-on. In this example, play the open first string. While the note is sounding, bring the ring finger (3) of your left hand down at the 3rd fret to play the second note without picking again.

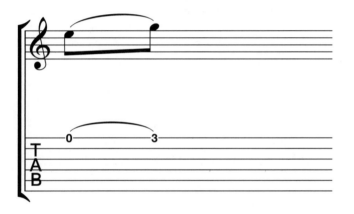

Pull-off

A slur connecting two descending notes indicates a pull-off. In this example, fret the first string with your ring finger (3) at the 3rd fret—then play the first note. While the note is ringing, pluck the string with your left-hand third finger to sound the open string.

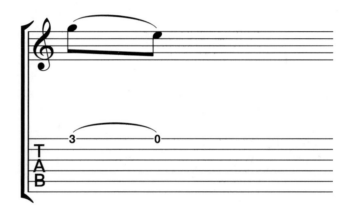

Slide

A slur and a diagonal line between two notes indicates a slide. In this example, fret the third string with your middle finger (2) at the 2nd fret. Then play the notes and quickly slide this finger up the string to the 4th fret. Slides can go up or down the neck.

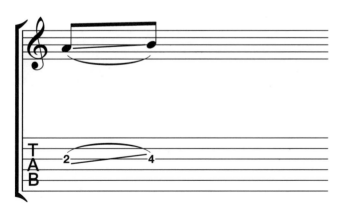

Bend

The curved arrow indicates a bend. In this example, fret the second string with your ring finger (3) at the 8th fret—and pick the first note. While the pitch is sounding, press the string up to bend the pitch up to the higher note—in this case, a tone higher.

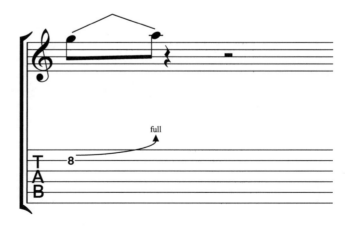

FILLS AND TURNAROUNDS

Now it's time to incorporate some lead guitar lines and the techniques from the previous page when playing blues songs, starting with fills and turnarounds.

A *fill* is a short instrumental section occurring at the end of vocal phrases in the blues.

A *turnaround* is a special type of fill used at the end of each verse, which leads naturally to the beginning of the next verse.

Here's a fill which is based on the minor pentatonic scale in the key of E. Use your middle finger (2) for notes on the 2nd fret and your ring finger (3) for notes on the 3rd fret. Play the fill, then strum the chord in the second bar.

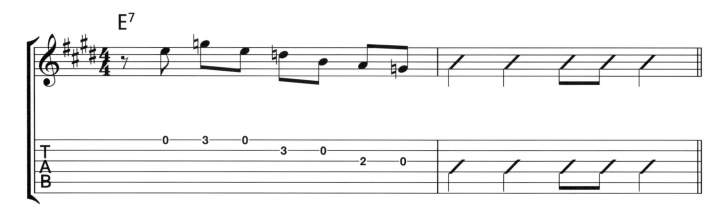

You can create many effective fills using the notes of the minor pentatonic scale. Here are two other useful fills in the key of E to practise.

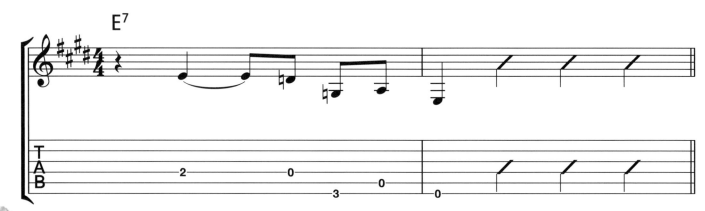

Most turnarounds use the V^7 chord during the last measure of a song to "turn around" the harmony and prepare our ears for the I chord at the beginning of the next verse. Play the E, Am and C chords, then strum this classic turnaround progression in the key of E.

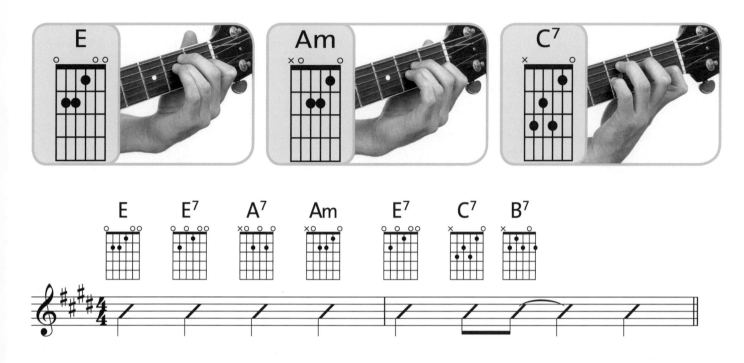

A turnaround usually includes a solo riff. Here's one in the key of E, which begins with a slide.

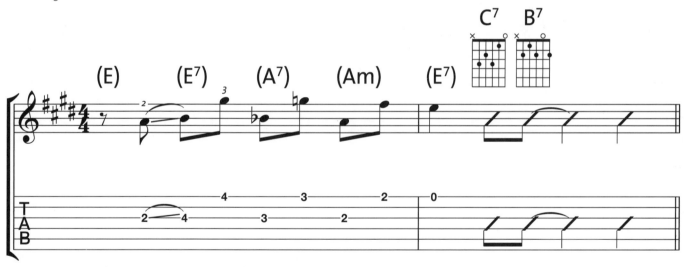

Alternative C7 shape

The change from C7 to B7 in these turnaround examples happens quite quickly. Many blues guitarists use a 'shortcut' shape in this context. Play C7 as a B7 shape a fret higher, and then slide down to B7.

Playing C7 this way won't stand up to scrutiny if the chord is to be held for any length of time (play the shape and strum it clearly to hear it properly). But in a turnaround where the chord is little more than an embellishment for B7, it'll sound fine.

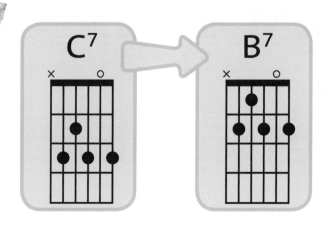

Now play 'Corinna, Corinna' with the indicated strums, fills, and turnarounds. This traditional blues has been recorded by many blues, country and swing artists—and became a chart hit for Ray Peterson in 1961.

Once you can play this blues smoothly as written, play the song a few more times and explore alternate fills and turnarounds (or make up some of your own). Write new discoveries down in a 'phrase book' for reference.

Corinna, Corinna

Cor - in - na, Cor - in - na, where you been so long?

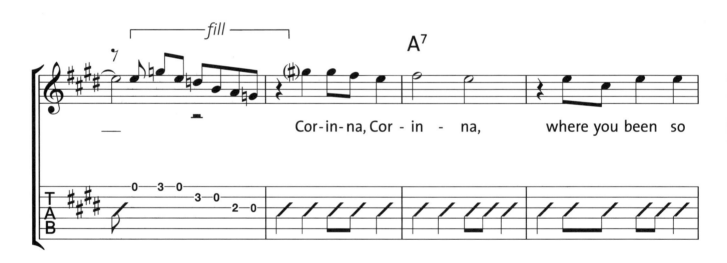

Cor - in - na, Cor - in - na, where you been so

long? I ain't had no lov - in' since you been gone.

INTROS AND ENDINGS

Traditional blues guitarists often play an instrumental introduction before the song begins. This is a nice place to do some solo work and establish the mood.

The classic blues intro echoes the harmony of the last line of the song itself. Here's an intro progression for a 12-bar blues in the key of A.

Strum this one now:

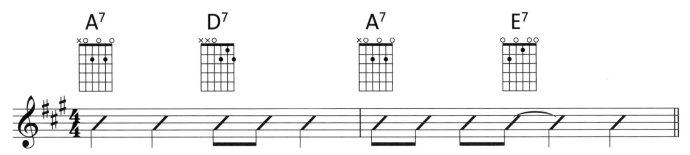

An intro usually includes a solo riff. Strum and play this intro in the key of A, which features a bluesy bend. The groups of three eighth notes are called triplets.

Play each group in the space of one beat to lend an easy-going shuffle feeling to this riff.

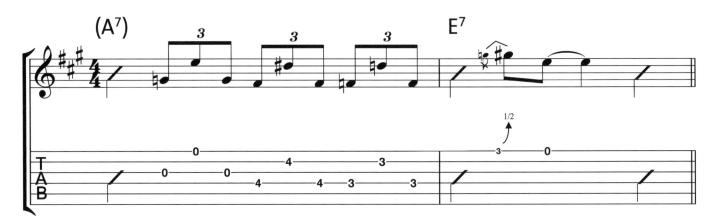

Here's another two-bar intro with a shuffle feel. To play this one, hold over the first notes of each triplet, as shown.

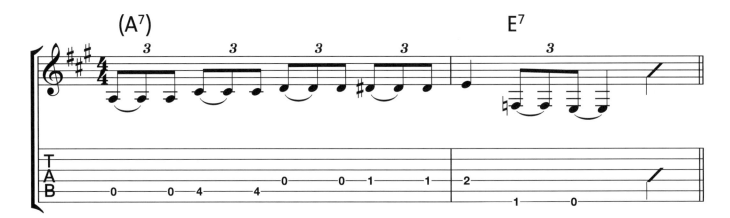

This rhythm is usually indicated as a quarter note and an eighth note grouped together with a triplet bracket.

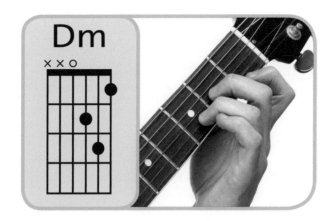

Most blues songs end with a two-measure chord progression, finishing on the I⁷ chord. Certain minor chords can be very effective in the typical blues ending.

Play the D minor chord, then strum this classic ending progression in the key of A.

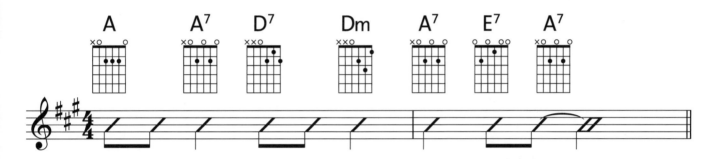

An ending can also include a solo riff. Strum and play this one in the key of A. Look out for the pull-off, hammer-on and slide in this riff.

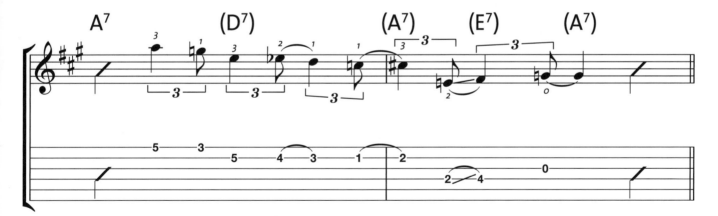

The shuffle rhythm can also be used when strumming chords. In fact, most blues songs are played with this easy-going feel.

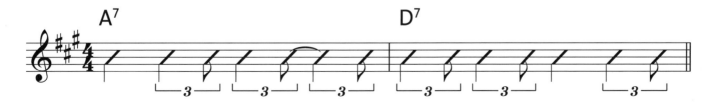

Now play 'Chilly Wind Blues' in a shuffle rhythm with the indicated intro and ending. The eighth note symbols at the top tells you to play each pair of eighth notes in the triplet pattern shown.

It allows the music to be written using standard eighth notes but played with a shuffle feel.

Once you can play 'Chilly Wind Blues' smoothly as written, play the song a few more times and invent your own intros and endings.

blow,   When I'm   gone   to my   long,   lone-some

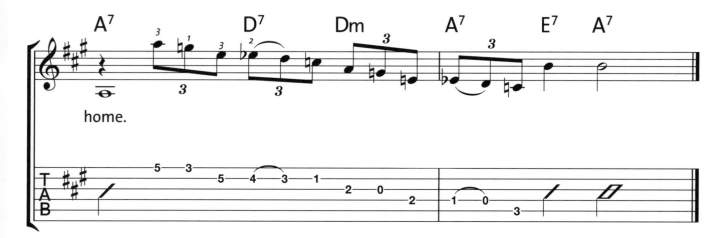

home.

2.
I'm goin' where the folks all know me well, my
sweet baby,
Goin' where the folks all know me well,
When I'm gone to my long, lonesome home.

3.
So, who will be your honey when I'm gone, my
sweet baby,
Who will be your honey when I'm gone,
When I'm gone to my long, lonesome home.

Versions of 'Chilly Wind Blues' have
been recorded by Odetta, Nina Simone,
Doc Watson and Papa Charlie Jackson.

SOLO TECHNIQUE

Blues guitarists usually include a full-verse solo in an arrangement of the song.

The harmonic pattern of the solo follows that of the song itself. Some solos even last for several verses.

The blues guitar solo is made up of different riffs that work well together as a whole. Most blues solos are based on the minor pentatonic scale.

Here is a pattern for a scale in A that moves up the neck.

Try playing each of these A pentatonic blues riffs now.

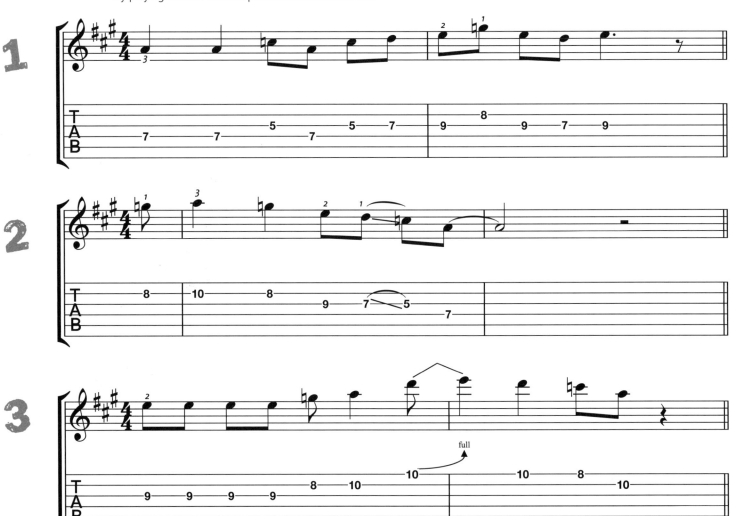

Once you can play these riffs, string them together into one twelve-bar section.

Here's how a 12-bar sequence might look, with chords, bar numbers, riffs and phrases (arched lines) shown:

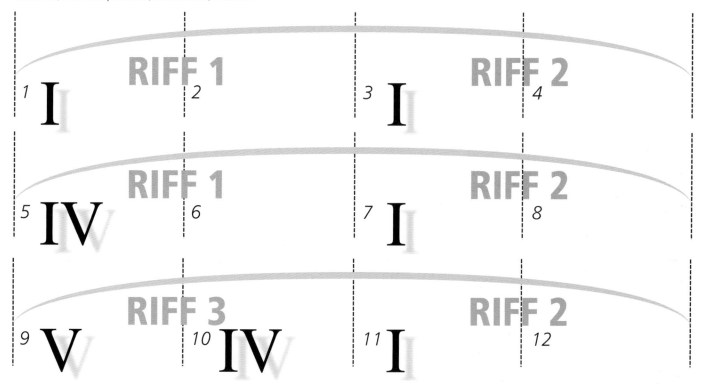

As you can see, riffs 1 and 2 are played over a I chord, riff 1 also works well with the IV chord, and riff 3 moves nicely from the V to the IV chords.

Because of the all-purpose nature of blues scales, many riffs are actually interchangeable. Here are two riffs that work equally well with both I and IV chords.

The short slides at the beginning of the first riff should start from one or two frets below the written note.

Now play 'Stagolee' in the key of A. Use the indicated strum, or your own variations, during the verse sections. Play the one-verse solo as written after verse 2 of the song, which uses the riffs from the previous pages.

Focus on increasing and decreasing your volume and expression to bring out each four-bar phrase—and to give the solo a definite beginning and ending.

You can play the solo again after verse 4, or create one of your own using a different combination of these riffs.

Stagolee solo

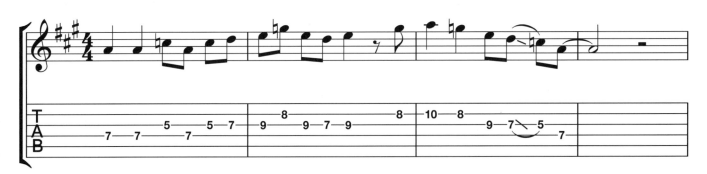

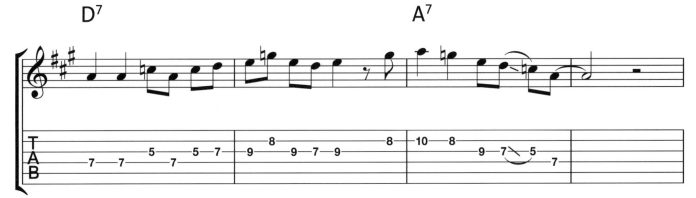

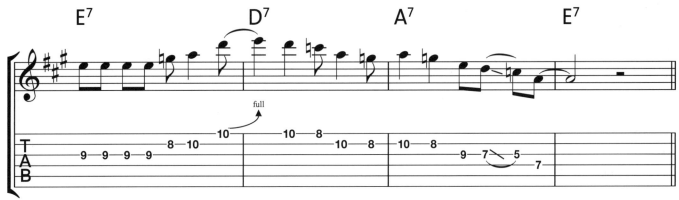

2.
Stagolee shot Billy Lyons—what do you think of that?
Shot him down in cold blood 'cause he stole his Stetson hat.
He was a bad man, cruel Stagolee.

(Solo)

3.
Billy Lyons said, "Stagolee, please don't take my life,
I've got two little babies and a darling, loving wife."
You are a bad man, cruel Stagolee.

4.
"What do I care for your babies or your darling, loving wife?
You done stole my Stetson—I'm bound to take your life."
He was a bad man, cruel Stagolee.

5.
Two o'clock next Tuesday, upon a scaffold high,
People came from miles around to watch old Stagolee die.
He was a bad man, cruel Stagolee.

'Stagolee' (also known as 'Stack-O-Lee Blues' or 'Stagger Lee') has been recorded by such greats such as Mississippi John Hurt, Woody Guthrie and Keb' Mo'.

IMPROVISING RIFFS

As we've seen, melodic passages in the blues are often based around the minor pentatonic scale. Let's take another look at the E minor pentatonic scale and explore some variations.

Here's the basic E minor pentatonic scale we first saw on page 14:

Now, let's add another note, known as the *flattened fifth*. In the key of E, it's B♭. Play through this scale, and hear the difference that the flattened fifth makes.

This note gives a more gritty character to the scale, making it even more suitable for the blues. In fact, this scale is known as the *blues scale*.

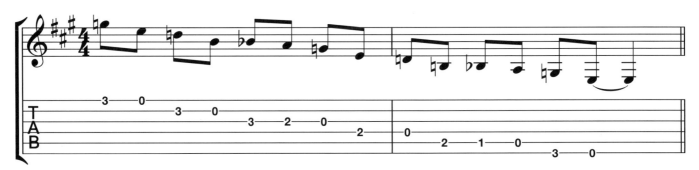

Finally, here's a variation that's often used in improvised solos. It contains all the notes of the blues scale (above), but with the addition of the *major third* (in this key, it's G♯). The blues scale already contains a *minor* third (in this key, it's G), and the major third provides a momentary release from the tense nature of the blues scale. Hear how moving up from the minor third to the major third adds brightness to the sound.

You could try bending up to the G♯, and experiment with making the bends slightly less than the full interval, to control the amount of tension you create.

In this version of the scale, the move is usually *from* the minor third *to* the major third, which is why the notes are written in the order below, despite the fact that the scale is descending.

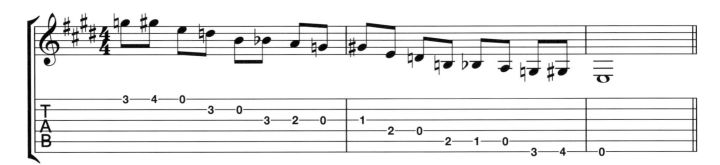

You can improvise many different kinds of riffs to complement the melody line of a given blues song.

In fact, many blues artists are known for their ability to weave the vocal and guitar lines together in this way.

Compare the first line of 'Midnight Special' with two riffs that are based on this melody. Note that the first riff imitates (or echoes) the vocal line. The second riff reverses (or mirrors) the vocal line. Both riffs make great fills that 'answer' the 'question' posed by the melody.

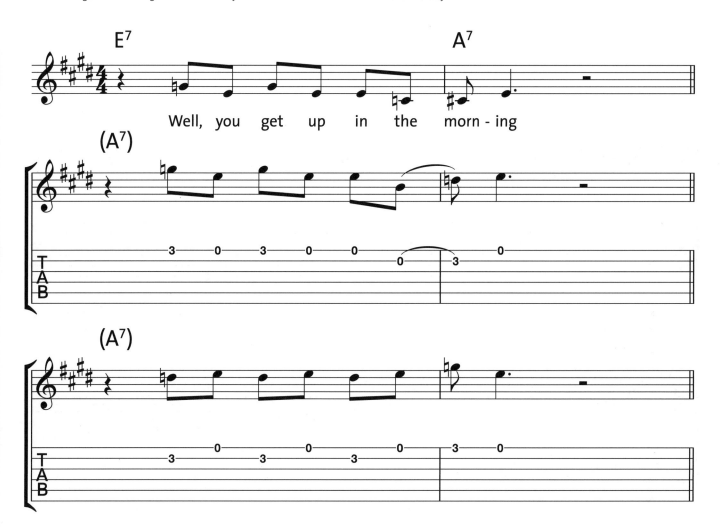

Some improvised riffs simply centre around special effects. This one uses slides and repeated notes.

Now play 'Midnight Special' (overleaf) using the indicated riffs. This old-time blues commemorates the midnight run of the *Golden Gate Limited*, whose engine headlight could be seen by inmates of the Texas State Prison.

This song uses an eight-bar blues form in a verse-verse-chorus pattern. Spend a moment looking through the arrangement to see how the scales are used. Notice, for example, the major thirds in bar 8, and the flattened fifth in bar 12.

Once you can play this arrangement smoothly, try improvising your own fills using the scales on page 28.

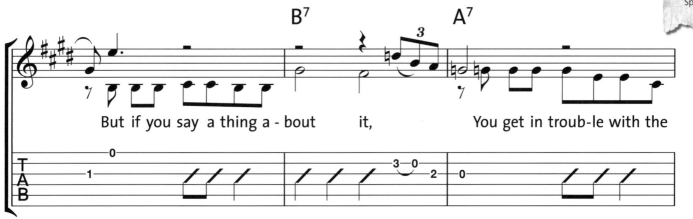

But if you say a thing a - bout it, You get in troub-le with the

Chorus

man. So, let the Mid - night Spe - cial,

Shine its light on me, Let the Mid-night Spe - cial,

Shine its ev-er-lov-in' light on___ me.

MINOR BLUES

So far you have played blues songs in major keys that contain a few minor chords. Blues songs written in a minor key feature minor chords primarily—and have a darkened mournful sound.

You are already familiar with the three basic chords in the key of A minor—Am, Dm and E7.

The F7 and C chord are also frequently used in the key of A minor.

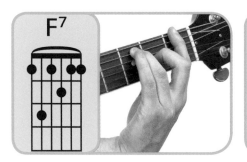 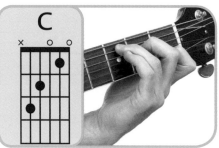 

The F7 chord shown above is called a *bar* chord, because you must use your index finger to fret all six strings at the 1st fret (in classical circles this is known as a *barre*).

The F chord shown may be easier to play and could be used in place of the F7 chord. However, it really pays to know both versions.

Once you're familiar with these chords, play 'St. James Infirmary', a traditional 8-bar minor blues. This grim tale of personal loss is a standard in the repertoire of blues and jazz musicians alike.

Explore the suggested intro, turnarounds, solo section, and ending as you develop your personal arrangement of this song. Bends, slides, hammer-ons and pull-offs add expression to the guitar solo, which works very nicely after verse 2 and/or verse 5.

You can improvise your own turnarounds and solos based on the A blues scale (which works equally well in major and minor keys).

You can easily find the basic chords of other minor keys in the *Table of Blues Chords* at the end of this book.

St. James Infirmary Blues

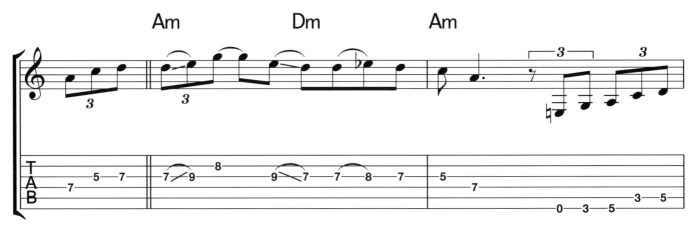

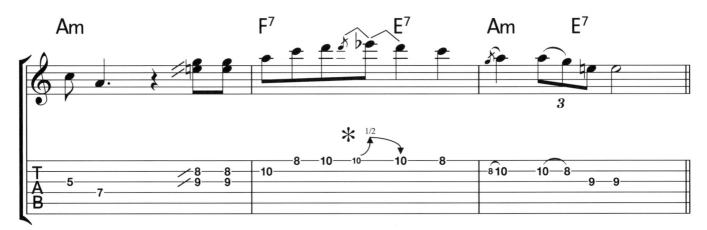

2.
I went down to see the doctor,
"She's very low," he said.
I went back to see my baby,
And, good God, she was lying there dead.

3.
I went down to Old Joe's bar-room,
On the corner by the square,
The drinks were served as usual,
And the usual crowd was there.

4.
On my left stood Joe MacKennedy,
His eyes were bloodshot red,
He turned to see the crowd around him,
And these are the words he said:

5.
Let her go, let her go, God bless her,
Wherever she may be.
She may search this wide world over,
But never find another man like me.

6.
Now when I die, please bury me
In a high-top Stetson hat,
Put a gold piece on my watch-chain,
So the gang will know I'm standing pat.

7.
And now that you've heard my story,
I'll take another shot of booze,
If anyone should happen to ask you,
I've got the St. James Infirmary blues.

*
Bend and release:
Notice the bends in bars 5 and 7 of the solo: the string is bent up
as usual, but is then *released* back down to the original pitch.

Turnarounds

Try either of these turnarounds at the indicated place in the song.

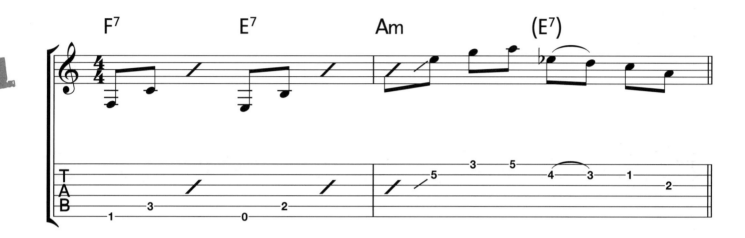

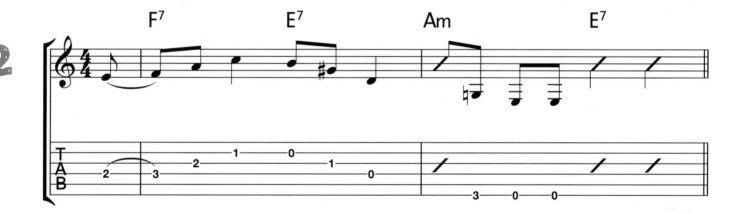

Ending

At the end of the song, try playing this instead of a turnaround.

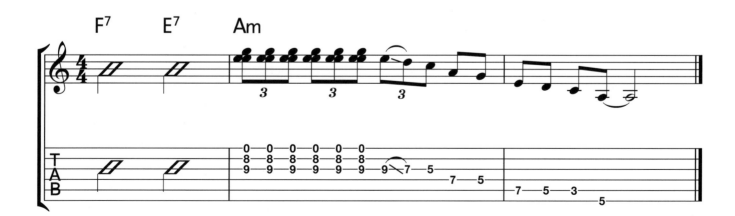

COUNTRY BLUES

The Mississippi Delta region was home to many early blues writers and musicians. As the blues spread through Texas and the South, it took on many characteristics of other existing Southern folk music.

This produced a wide range of regional styles, collectively known as country blues. Finger picking is an important playing technique for many country blues guitarists.

So let's take a peek at blues finger picking styles. You'll never look back!

Here's how the fingers are named (below):

This naming convention comes from classical guitar, and stretches right back to lute music from the Renaissance. In folk styles such as the blues, you'll sometimes see 't' for thumb, but this system is still widely used. The 'p' is for *pulgar*, 'i' for *indio*, 'm' is *medio*, and 'a' is *annular*.

Notice that there's no name for the little finger. Although a name exists ('c' for *chiquita*) it's very rarely used, as the little finger generally doesn't get a look-in.

The following exercises use these three chord shapes, so take a quick look at them now:

  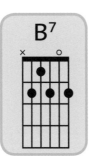

Letters in the notation show which right-hand finger picks the string.

To play this style, you must keep a steady bassline going with your thumb while holding the chord shapes shown:

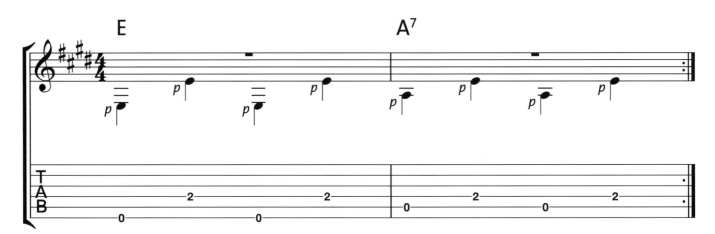

Now try adding some treble notes. The first note in each measure falls on the beat and, along with the first bass note, is called the pinch.

The other two notes fall in between beats. Try accenting them to create a *syncopated* feel—off-beat accents add rhythmic interest in a style approaching ragtime.

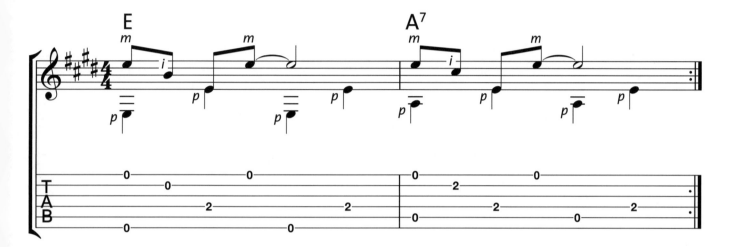

You can get a different country feel by adding thumb brushes to the alternating bass pattern.

To get this effect, just brush down across two or three strings instead of playing a single bass note on beats 2 and 4 of the bass line (a thumb brush is indicated by an arrow next to the brushed notes). Brushing the lower notes with the thumb will create a slightly fuller sound—but don't overdo it!

Use thumb brushes as you play this pattern, moving from an A7 chord to a B7 chord. The brackets indicate optional notes—notes that are already picked with the fingers, but which might also sound with the thumb brushes.

Experiment with the extent of the brushes to create a contrast between the bass (thumb) notes and the upper (picked) notes of the chord.

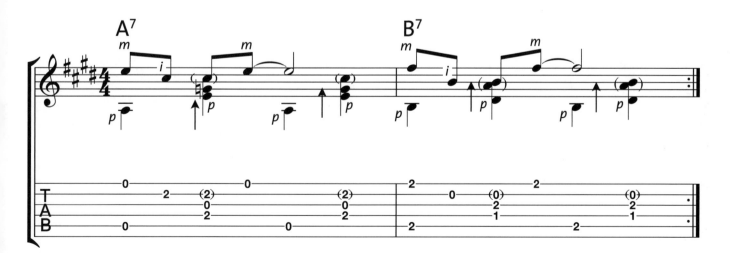

Now play 'Risin' River Blues' using this pattern.

Notice that variations on this picking pattern are used in the introduction and ending of this traditional country blues to add movement and interest to the arrangement. Experiment with accents: emphasise the off-beat melody notes for a more syncopated feel.

Risin' River Blues

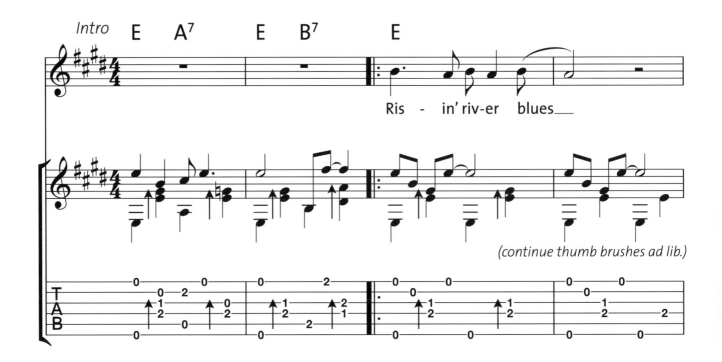

(continue thumb brushes ad lib.)

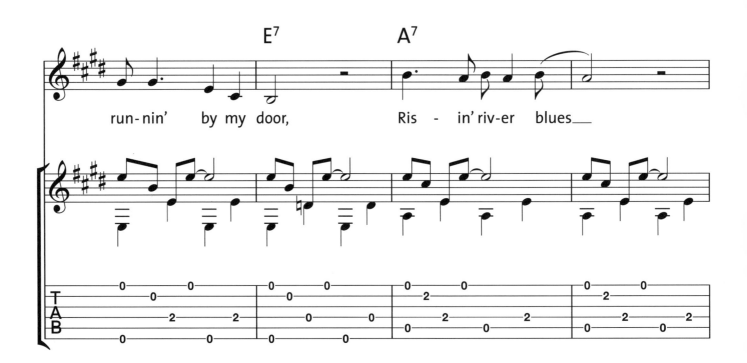

Come here, sweet mama, let me speak my mind,
Come here, sweet mama, let me speak my mind,
To cure these blues, gonna take a long, long time.

JAZZ BLUES

Jazz developed in the early part of the last century as a natural extension of the blues. In fact, many early jazz tunes were nothing more than a blues song with an expanded structure and harmony.

For example the 'St. Louis Blues' (pages 42-43) is written in three sections—and requires several new chords in the key of G, as shown below.

Practise each of these chords until you can change smoothly from one to another.

The typical jazz blues song requires a more sophisticated chord progression than the traditional blues form.

These additional chords gave the jazz blues song that characteristic ragtime sound and helped the song to sustain a larger overall structure.

A favourite number of Louis Armstrong and other jazz performers, this sophisticated jazz blues features a powerful chromatic melody line and some interesting syncopated rhythms. On the next page, we'll take a look at some strumming suggestions that will provide contrast and interest throughout the song.

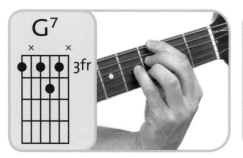

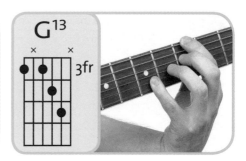

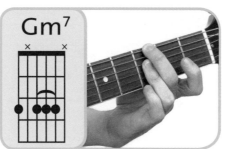

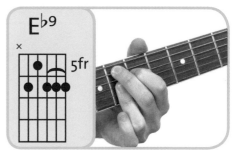

Listen to versions recorded by Bessie Smith (1925), Johnny Dodds (1927), Louis Armstrong (1929) and Django Reinhardt (1937), among others.

W.C. Handy (sometimes called "the father of the blues") wrote the music and lyrics to 'St. Louis Blues' in 1914. Since then, this song has enjoyed worldwide popularity—and even inspired a musical film of the same name in 1928 featuring Bessie Smith.

Strumming styles

'St. Louis Blues' has sections that feature different musical styles. W.C. Handy's compositional style stemmed from ragtime music, which often had contrasting sections, and Handy extended this idea to many of his blues compositions.

Famously, 'St. Louis Blues' contains an opening ballad section, reminiscent of of the mournful New Orleans jazz funeral style; next, there's a section that reflects the contemporary tango fashion—this might seem incongruous to our ears, but this feature made the piece very popular with dancers at the time; and finally we move to a 'low-down' blues: a heavily rhythmic closing section.

Let's look at ways to create strumming effects for each of the different styles.

For the intro and verse, try picking each chord once with the thumb and three fingers together: this is a typical technique for jazz guitar, where most shapes only use four strings.

You might try playing the strings in quick succession starting with the thumb, so there's a slight ripple effect.

Where the chord contains more than four notes, such as the C9, you'll simply need to make a choice about which string to omit—or brush across the strings with the thumb instead.

Intro

In the bridge, to acheive the rigid, detached feel of the tango beat, strum each chord forcefully on the beat, immediately bringing the strumming hand to rest on the strings.

Muting the strings this way straight after the strum will create a staccato rhythm of crisp, separate chords. For the full dramatic effect, dig in to the strings slightly to prolong the strum:

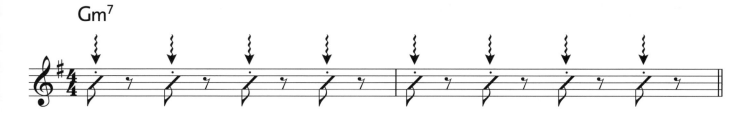

Finally, in the chorus, the tempo picks up to a medium-paced swing feel. Strum swung eighths—that is, with a triplet feel—like so:

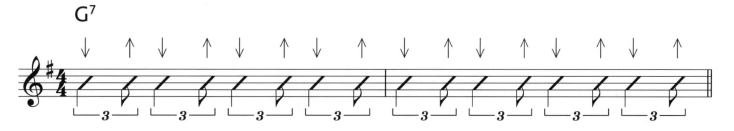

St. Louis Blues

Intro

Verse

I hate to see__ the eve-nin' sun go down,
Feel-in' to-mor-row like__ I feel to - day,

Hate to see__ the eve-nin' sun go down.
Feel to - mor - row like__ I feel to - day.

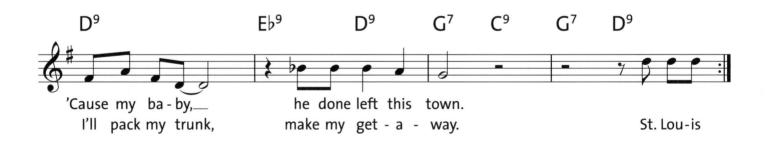

'Cause my ba - by,__ he done left this town.
I'll pack my trunk, make my get - a - way. St. Lou-is

Bridge

wom-an_____ with her dia-mond rings, Pulls that

BLUES ROCK

Rock 'n' roll owes its heritage to the blues. In fact, many rock artists have created popular hits using traditional blues songs. 'Crossroads Blues' was a favourite of blues master Robert Johnson. In 1969, Cream did a classic blues-rock version of this great 12-bar blues. For the intro and fill sections of 'Crossroads', Eric Clapton plays a similar riff to the one shown here, made up of notes taken from a first-position A minor pentatonic scale. Try this now:

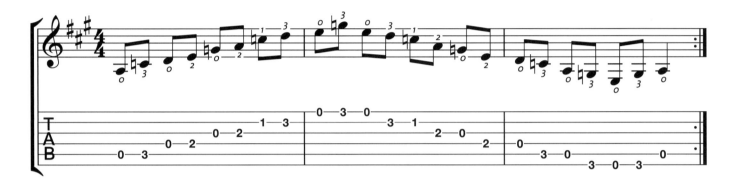

Now play this riff, which features a pull-off followed by a hammer-on. Fret the A note on the third string at the 2nd fret using your second finger.

Play the note, and then pull off the strings with your left-hand 2nd finger to sound the open third string. Now replace your 2nd finger on the third string at the 2nd fret to play the third note.

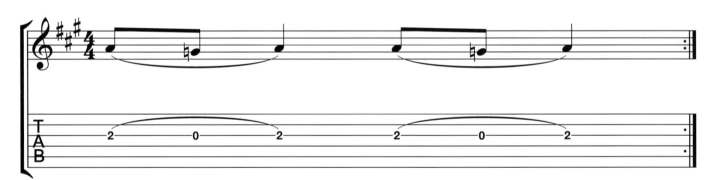

Now try the whole riff. If you are playing with a pick, use down-strokes (⊓) and up-strokes (Ⅴ) as indicated.

If you're playing with your fingers, use your thumb to play the low A note on the open fifth string and pick the treble notes with alternating index and middle fingers.

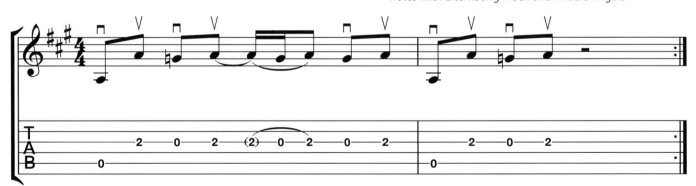

The solo in 'Crossroads' (page 47) makes use of the blues scale we saw on page 28. This time it's an A blues, and here (page 45) it's written from the A on the bottom string all the way up to the 12th fret on the top string, and back down again. The E blues and A blues scales are probably the most common scales for improvising blues solos.

At the beginning of the solo, you'll see a wavy line above the whole-note A (10th fret, second string). This symbol indicates *vibrato*.

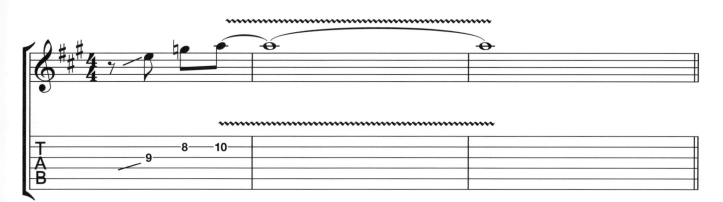

As you hold a note, shake your hand back and forth in line with the guitar neck. This produces a slight variation in pitch and intensity of the held note. For a more pronounced type of vibrato, you can shake your finger up and down, perpendicular to the neck. Experiment with these two types of vibrato at different speeds and levels of intensity as you're learning this blues-rock solo.

Try coming up with your own intro, fills and solo for 'Crossroads'. Experiment with mixing the two scale forms and finding the right places for hammer-ons, pull-offs, slides, bends and vibrato. Feel free to make a note of the riffs that work best as you put together your own blues-rock arrangement of this classic song.

Crossroads Blues

Fast

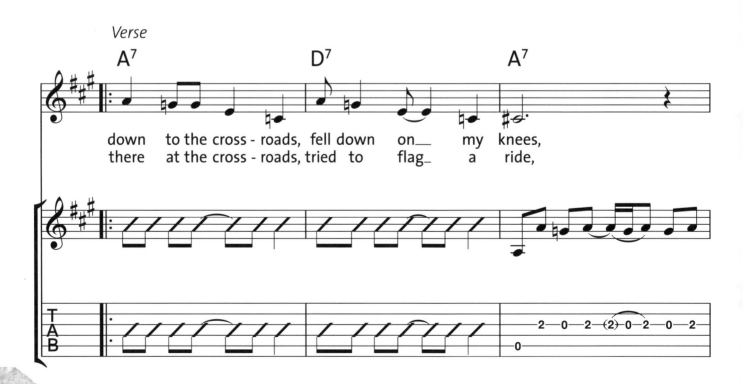

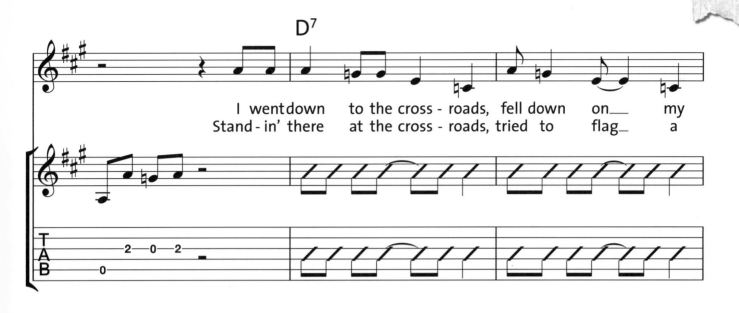

I went down to the cross - roads, fell down on___ my
Stand - in' there at the cross - roads, tried to flag___ a

knees,
ride,

I asked the Lord to have mer - cy,
No - bo - dy there seemed to know me,

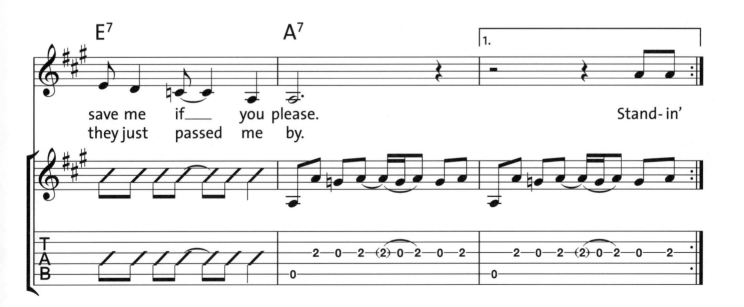

save me if___ you please.
they just passed me by.

Stand-in'

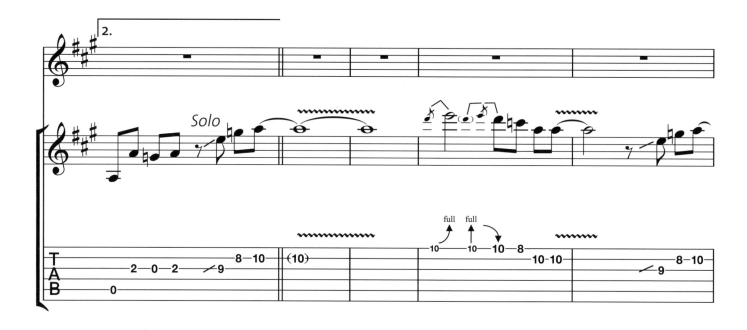

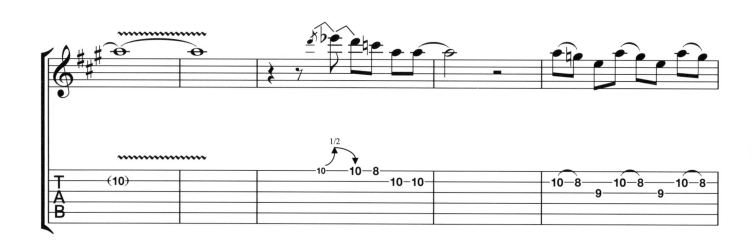

BLUES SEQUENCES

The following pages contain blues scales in every key (pages 50–53), as well as the most commonly used blues chords in every major and minor key (pages 54–55).

Here are some basic progressions you can use to play different versions of the blues in the key of your choice. Firstly, some common structures for blues, which you should be familiar with:

Standard 8-Bar Blues

I	I^7	IV	I	
V^7	V^7	I IV^7	I	

Standard 12-Bar Blues

I	I	I	I^7	
IV^7	IV^7	I	I	
V^7	V^7	I	I	

12-Bar Blues Variation

I	IV^7	I	I^7	
IV^7	IV^m	I	I^7	
V^7	IV^7	I	I	

Minor 12-Bar Blues

I^{m7}	I^{m7}	I^{m7}	I^{m7}	
IV^m	IV^m	I^m	I^{m7}	
V^7	IV^m	I^{m7}	I^{m7}	

Minor 12-Bar Blues Variation

I^{m7}	IV^m V^7	I^{m7}	I^7	
IV^m	IV^m V^9	I^{m7}	I^7	
IV^m	♭VI^7 V^9	I^{m7}	I^{m7}	

Use these two-measure progressions to play a basic blues intro, turnaround, or ending in any major key.

Intro
I	♭VI^7	V^7	

Turnaround
I I^7	IV IV^m	I ♭VI^7 V^7	

Ending
I	IV^7 ♭VI^7	I I^7	

Use these two-measure progressions to play a basic blues intro, turnaround, or ending in any minor key.

Intro
I^{m7} IV^m	V^7 ♭VI^7 V^7	

Turnaround
I^m I^{m7} IV^m ♭VI^7	V^7 ♭VI^7 V^7	

Ending
I^{m7} IV^m V^9	I^{m7}	

BLUES SCALE DIRECTORY

This section shows fingering for the blues scale in every key.

As a general rule, blues guitarists favour the keys of A, E, D, and G. However, you may need to transpose a given song on the spot when you're working with other musicians.

BLUES CHORDS BY KEY

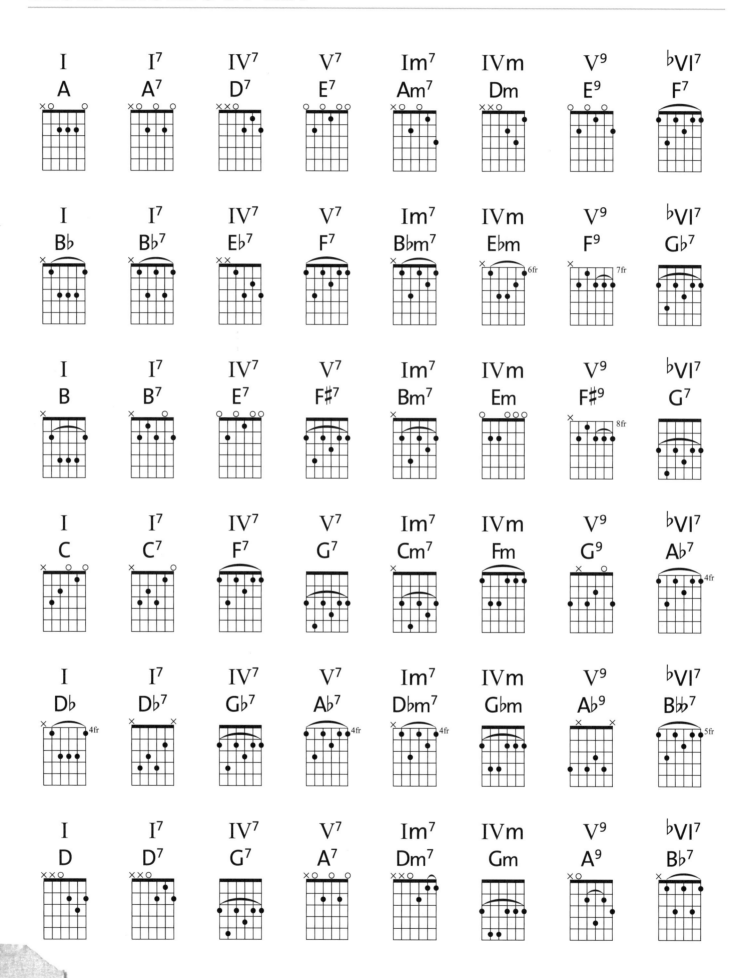

I	I⁷	IV⁷	V⁷	Im⁷	IVm	V⁹	♭VI⁷
E♭	E♭⁷	A♭⁷	B♭⁷	E♭m⁷	A♭m	B♭⁹	C♭⁷
E	E⁷	A⁷	B⁷	Em⁷	Am	B⁹	C⁷
F	F⁷	B♭⁷	C⁷	Fm⁷	B♭m	C⁹	D♭⁷
F#	F#⁷	B⁷	C#⁷	F#m⁷	Bm	C#⁹	D⁷
G	G⁷	C⁷	D⁷	Gm⁷	Cm	D⁹	E♭⁷
A♭	A♭⁷	D♭⁷	E♭⁷	A♭m⁷	D♭m	E♭⁹	F♭⁷

Your Guarantee of Quality

As publishers, we strive to produce every book
to the highest commercial standards.

This book has been carefully designed to minimise awkward
page turns and to make playing from it a real pleasure.

Particular care has been given to specifying acid-free, neutral-sized
paper made from pulps which have not been elemental chlorine bleached.
This pulp is from farmed sustainable forests and was produced with
special regard for the environment.

Throughout, the printing and binding have been planned to
ensure a sturdy, attractive publication which should give years of enjoyment.

If your copy fails to meet our high standards,
please inform us and we will gladly replace it.

1 2 3 4 5 6 7 8 9